Wish's Derby

Carl O'Callaghan

Photography by
Kenny Sanchez, Barbara Livingston,
Terri Crookham, John Chun,
Cecilia Gustavsson, Hector Cuevas,
and Michelle McDonald

ISBN: 1483978478
ISBN 13: 9781483978475
Library of Congress Control Number: 2013905998
CreateSpace Independent Publishing Platform
North Charleston, South Carolina

Dedication

So at this time in writing, I would like to dedicate this book to Kinsale King, my horse; to his great owners Dr.'s Patrick and Arlene G. Sheehy, to all of Wish Upon a Teen staff in Michigan with special thanks to Michelle Soto and her son Zachary, who inspire me everyday. To Jamie Greene Kaniarz who helped me put my story into writing and last but not least, my parents, family, friends, and all of you reading this book. Together we can make a difference in many teens' lives.

For more information, please visit them at www.wishuponateen.org

Carl O'Callaghan is possibly one of the best-known names in the world of horse Racing. A featured face at Royal Ascot, Breeders Cup and the Golden Jubilee, Carl is a force to be reckoned with. Carl has traveled all over the world from Dubai to England and all the US in search of his dream, which is horse racing. Carl also became one of the youngest trainers to win the 2 million dollar sprint in his first year of training in Dubai; and Wish Upon a Teen is lucky to have Carl bringing his compassion and dedication he is famous for to Wish Upon a Teen as one of our Celebrity Ambassador.

Letter From The Author

Well another chapter in my crazy life "ha ha". My teachers from Newmarket, Fergus, and St Caminis back home in Ireland must be in shock; as here I am writing a book for kids. They all know I was never a kid for school work (thank goodness for spell check and computers). I've always preferred to be outside doing something fun as I am today, training horses. But, if not for all my school teachers, my friends and family I would not be where I am today, so thank you for that. Now let me take a chance to thank some people, as this is what this page is for, (so I'm told). First, thank you to the best mother in the world who raised me and my brother to be very strong people and always stood behind us with the choices we made in life. When I decided to come to America in 1990 at the age of 14, my mom knew she would miss me but also knew I was going for the right reasons and that was to follow my dreams with horses, HINT that's why and how I'm writing this book. I'd like thank Clinton my brother for always trying to understand that all I love is horses, but I'm also proud of him because he also helps kids with autism in a program called Surf to Heel back in Ireland. A lot of people ask why do I do this, well from my point of view I don't know but I can tell you from the time I can remember my mom was always a helper and a giver and still is and I think both my brother and I get that from her so once again MOM thank you. From the bottom of my heart I Love You! Now, thank you to all the people I have worked with and worked for since I was young from back home to the USA. You have all touched me in some way or another, to all the friends I have met since living in the US thank you. To a man named Dr. Frank Sheehy and his family and all my clients for giving me a training career back in 2009 and for Dr. Sheehy giving that famous horse who brought all our dreams to come true, Kinsale King. This book is about King and I, with a little twist of humor, (humor I mean I'm talking for the animals). I also want to thank my dad for giving me the gift of music which I love as a hobby and enjoy as a past time. To all my staff I work with day in and day out thank you, and most importantly thank you to all the kids I've met on this journey and hope to meet more. A huge Thank You to Wish Upon a Teen and their team based in Michigan. I hope my story of my horse King and my goat Ruben will tell the story that it's ok to be different and that the people close to us Love us very much........

Ps. Thank you Kinsale King for changing my life, I love you!

Kenny Sanchez

Barbara Livingston

Terri Crookham

Cecilia Gustavsson

Michelle McDonald

John Chun

Hector Cuevas

Drawing by: Drew Zimmerman

Everyone at Irish Stables was
preparing for the big Woodward Derby.

Everybody, that is, except for Wish.

Wish had been at Irish Stables since he was 4 years old. He loved it there, but lately everyone has been in a tizzy, training for the big derby. Wish tries to focus on the work at hand and follow directions, but sometimes it just gets to be too much with all the trainers constantly shouting commands.

"Walk over here!"
"Turn around over there!"
"Look up!"
"Look down!"
"Trot."
"Trot!"
"Trot!"

Frankly, sometimes it's just too much for Wish to handle. He feels overloaded, and he feels stressed. Some days, he feels like he just needs to curl up by himself and turn off everything in his head.

The trainers all look at Wish and say, "Wish would be such a great racing horse, if only he could follow directions and listen to us."

The other horses make fun of Wish for this. Axel, a big horse who likes to tease, says things to Wish that make him feel sad and gloomy.

"What's wrong with you, Wish?"
"Why can't you just follow directions like the rest of us?"
"Why don't you look at us when we are talking to you?"
"Why don't you laugh at our jokes?"
"Why are you just so *WEIRD*?"

These comments made Wish feel terrible, and all alone. When Axel and the other horses train together and hang out in the stable afterward, playing horseshoes, eating carrots and telling jokes with each other, Wish would just lay off to the side, all by himself.

"Everyone else has friends except for me," Wish told his only friend, Ruben. "No one wants to work with me, and I am just no good at racing. I am just so *WEIRD*!"

Ruben was the resident stable goat.

"Oh Wish, there is nothing wrong with you!" Ruben said, "if you think you're sore or your legs hurt and you are worried that you can't race, then lift up your leg and show it to Carl in the morning when he comes to your stable. You might just have a sore foot that he could fix in no time."

"Some might think you're QUIRKY because you think too much, and that's okay, we all have different ways of thinking and doing things."

"What does that mean?" Wish asked.

"It means that your mind works a different way", Ruben said. "And sometimes it is hard for you to do things the same way as the other horses. You just have to do it your own way."

Wish started to ask Ruben why the other horses were so mean to him, when suddenly they heard a commotion from the other side of the stable. Wish and Ruben saw all the trainers and other horses running into the training ring, so they ran too.

When they arrived to the center ring and saw what was happening, Wish was shocked. "Oh no!" he cried.

Ruben agreed. "This is very bad."

Axel had tripped during his training and cut his leg! He would have to rest for weeks in order to let it heal. This meant that he would not be able to run in the Woodward Derby.

Everyone was quiet and in a bad mood at Irish Stables for the rest of the day. Axel had been training very hard and was predicted to win the Woodward Derby, but now it looked like the stables would not even have a horse to race.

The next morning, Wish heard his name being called. He wondered what was going on and who was calling him. "Wish, it's time to wake up; we've got some training to do."

It was Carl, the head trainer! He and Ruben had come to see Wish.

"Aye," said Carl, "Ruben and I were having a talk last night during tea, and we decided that you should run in Axel's place in the Woodward Derby and represent Irish Stables."

"WHAT?!? Me??" Wish thought. "No, I can't I have a sore foot, and unless I soak it in hot water today and fix it, I won't be able to run fast." As if Carl knew what Wish was thinking, he started to pat Wish and said, "don't worry about a thing, I will fix that foot and you will feel like a new kid again and then we will train together."

Over the next few days, Carl and Wish worked hard and trained all day. Whenever Wish felt overwhelmed or scared, Carl let him take a break and gather up his thoughts before training more. Ruben was there all day, every day, to cheer them on.

As Wish trained with Carl, the other horses started to realize what a great racehorse he was. They all realized that Wish was very fast and that he actually might have a chance at winning the Woodward Derby. They stopped calling him quirky and weird and instead started complimenting him on his fast running. They really thought he could do it!

Finally, the big day was here. As Wish was getting ready for the derby, Carl and Ruben came to give him a pep talk. "Come on, Wish, you can do this," said Ruben.

"I want you to go out there and run like you have never run before," Carl told Wish. "No matter what, I want you to know that I am proud of you and your hard work."

"I brought you a present," Carl told Wish. He reached into his backpack and pulled out a blanket.

"This is my lucky racing blanket," Carl explained to Wish. "I always put it under the saddle of the horses I train. It brings them luck."
As Carl unrolled the blanket, Wish thought he saw his name. As he looked closer, he realized his name wasn't the only thing written on the blanket.

"Wish Upon a Teen," Carl read the words out loud. "Wish Upon a Teen is a nonprofit that I work with. They help quirky teens learn how to succeed on their own terms, just like you did, Wish. You always had it in you to be a great runner; you just needed someone to believe in you and to give you the tools that you needed."

With that being said, the speakers boomed, "Horses and jockeys to the starting line!"

Carl and Ruben told Wish good luck.

As Wish and his jockey, and long time friend, prepared to race, Wish could feel his blood pumping. "Here we go!" thought Wish.

And away they GO!

Wish thought he had never run so fast in his life. He was running so fast, everything else seemed to be a blur; he could not even slow down enough to turn his head to the side to see if any other horse was close to him or even right next to him.

In the blink of an eye, it was over.

18

Wish looked around, expecting to see all
the other horses who had beaten him to the
finish line, but he did not see anyone.
"Oh no," thought Wish. "I took so long to run the
derby, everyone else has already finished and left."
Then he heard Carl's voice, yelling above all the noise.
"I did not mean to let you down, Carl," Wish thought.

But Carl did not look angry; in fact, he was
smiling. Yes, he had a *huge* smile on his face.

"I knew you could do it, Wish. I just knew it!" Carl said. Wish looked around just as another horse came across the same finish line that Wish had crossed just moments ago; that horse was followed by six other horses right behind him.

"What!" thought Wish, "I didn't lose—wait a minute. I won!"

At that moment the speaker started to announce the winners. Wish listened for his name and for Irish Stables.

They announced third place, then second place, and finally the announcer said, "In first place, the winner of the Woodward Derby, from Irish Stables: *Wish*!"

Wish watched as Carl and Ruben
danced as his name was called.

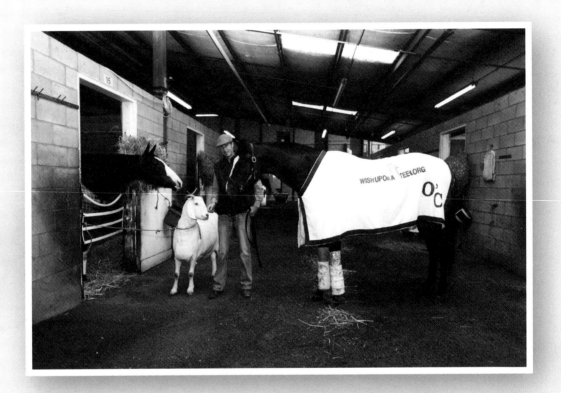

"I did it!" Wish thought, "and all because someone
believed in me and took his time to help me."

22